SUPER Stomach

and the digestive system

JOURNEY THROUGH
the
Human
BODY

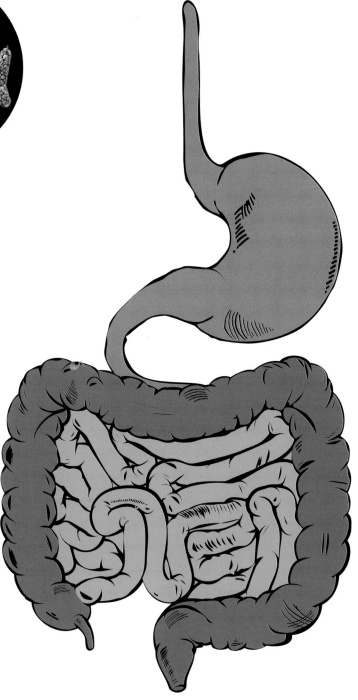

By
Charlie Ogden

Designed by Danielle Jones

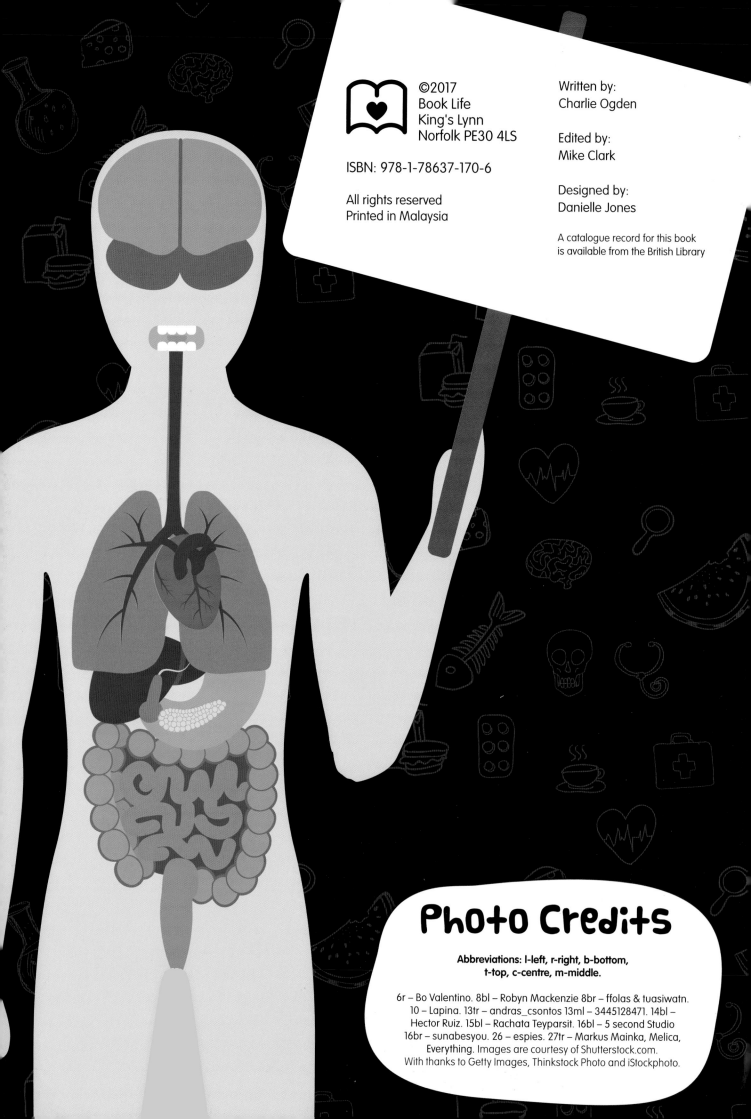

©2017
Book Life
King's Lynn
Norfolk PE30 4LS

ISBN: 978-1-78637-170-6

All rights reserved
Printed in Malaysia

Written by:
Charlie Ogden

Edited by:
Mike Clark

Designed by:
Danielle Jones

A catalogue record for this book
is available from the British Library

Photo Credits

**Abbreviations: l-left, r-right, b-bottom,
t-top, c-centre, m-middle.**

SUPER Stomach
and the digestive system

CONTENTS

Words that look like **this** are explained in the glossary on page 31.

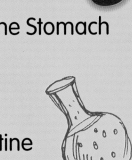

Hi, I'm Dr. Tommy Ake. Follow me to start your journey through the digestive system!

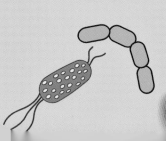

The HUMAN BODY

The human body is very complicated. The body is full of **organs**, bones, **muscles** and blood and all of these parts are wrapped up in a thin layer of skin. Because of this, finding your way around the human body can be very difficult anddangerous if you don't have a guide.

TO THE DIGESTIVE SYSTEM

But lucky for you, I am here – so let our journey begin!

HUMAN BODY

MAP

There are over **75 ORGANS** in the **HUMAN BODY!**

Systems of the Body

The first thing that you need to know about the human body is that it uses **systems**. The systems of the body are made up of groups of organs that work together.

Each system of the body has its own important job to do, such as stopping the body from getting sick or helping to keep the body strong.

There are lots of different systems in the body, but some are more important than others. Four of the most important systems in the body are:

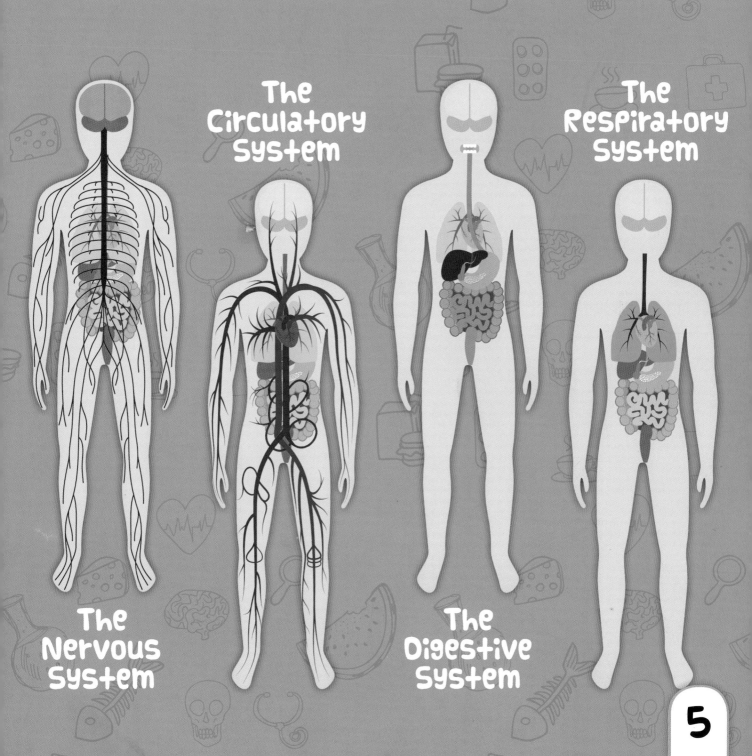

The
Circulatory
System

The
Respiratory
System

The
Nervous
System

The
Digestive
System

The DIGESTIVE SYSTEM

The digestive system is possibly the most complicated system in the whole body! This is because it involves lots of different organs and these organs have to work together in lots of different ways.

The digestive system also uses glands. Glands are organs that produce things that help the body to grow or stay healthy. There are glands around the eyes that make tears and glands in the armpit that make sweat.

YOU'RE IN SAFE GLANDS

A gland in this part of the eye makes tears. Tears help to keep the eye clean.

Glands in the armpit make sweat. Sweat helps to keep the body cool.

THE FOOD TUBE

Most of the digestive system is made up of a long tube that stretches from the mouth to the rectum. This tube is made up of lots of organs that are long and thin. The organs are shaped like this because it makes it easier for food to move through them. This long tube is called the digestive tract.

There are other organs in the digestive system that are not a part of the digestive tract. These organs either make or store the juices that are needed for the digestive system to work.

ORGAN-ISATION

This diagram shows all of the different organs in the digestive system and where in the body they can be found.

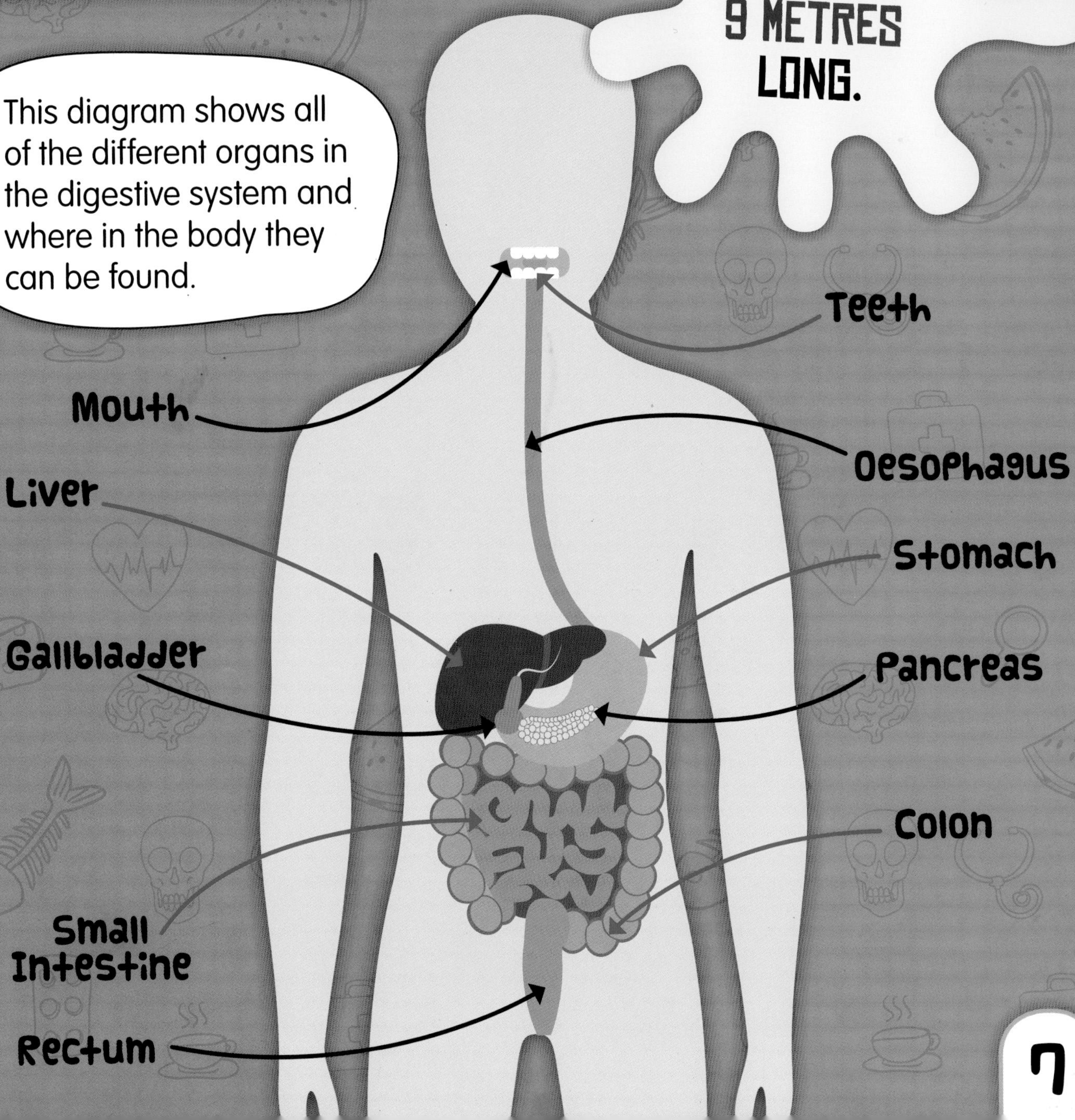

An adult's **DIGESTIVE TRACT** is over **9 METRES LONG.**

Teeth

Mouth

Oesophagus

Liver

Stomach

Gallbladder

Pancreas

Colon

Small Intestine

Rectum

YOU ARE What YOU EAT

The digestive system is very important. It breaks down food into things that the body needs and then **absorbs** these things so that they can be used by the body. As soon as food enters the mouth, the digestive system gets to work getting all of the **nutrients** out of it. These nutrients do loads of great things for the body - they help the body to grow, they help the body to repair itself and they give the body energy!

THE NEED FOR FEED

Different types of food help the body to do different things. Different types of food are known as food groups.

The process of **BREAKING DOWN food** and **ABSORBING** the **NUTRIENTS** is called **DIGESTION.**

Meat and fish are both a part of the protein food group. Foods in this group contain lots of protein, which helps to repair the body and its organs.

Bread and rice are both a part of the **carbohydrates** food group. Foods in this group are the body's main source of energy, so it is important to eat carbohydrates at every meal.

WASTE NOT, WANT NOT

The digestive system also has another important job – getting rid of waste. While the digestive system is great at getting all of the useful nutrients out of food, there are lots of things in food that the body doesn't need. Rather than absorbing these things, the digestive system gets rid of them in the form of poo. This process is called excretion.

Doctors have lots of different names for **POO**, including FAECES, STOOL, WASTE and EXCREMENT.

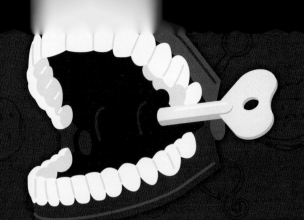

SINK YOUR TEETH into this

Welcome to the first stop on our tour – the teeth! The teeth are a very important part of the digestive system, so be sure to take good care of yours.

Before any food can enter the human digestive system, it almost always has to come into contact with the teeth. The teeth are used to chew food before it is swallowed, which helps to break the food down and make it easier to digest.

Look out for these signs. The pink section shows you where we are in the body!

ARMED TO THE TEETH

Humans have three main types of teeth, each of which has their own job to do.

Incisors

The teeth at the front of the mouth are called incisors. These teeth are thin and sharp and are used to cut food into small chunks.

Canines

The pointed teeth on either side of the incisors are called canines. These teeth are used to rip off pieces of tough food, such as meat.

Molars

The teeth farthest back in the mouth are called the molars. These teeth are used to grind food into small pieces.

WATCH YOUR MOUTH

You may think that the digestion process starts when food enters the mouth, but you would be wrong. The mouth starts the digestion process before the food has even touched the lips.

SHE NOSE WHAT EYE AM THINKING

The mouth teams up with the nose, the eyes and the brain to get the digestion process started before any food has even entered the mouth. If the nose smells something tasty, or if the eyes see something delicious, or if the brain even thinks of something yummy, then the mouth starts to make **saliva**.

This shows where the three main glands are in the mouth. These glands all make saliva.

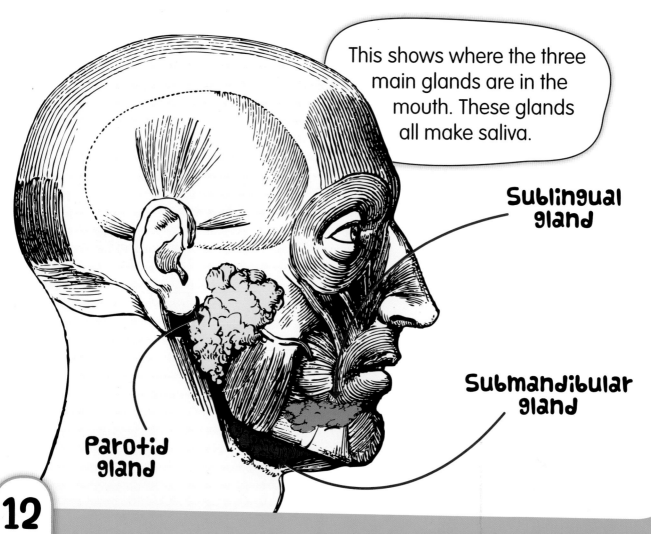

Sublingual gland

Submandibular gland

Parotid gland

Saliva has two main jobs in the digestion process. The first one is easy – it makes food wet. Wet food is easier to swallow and is less likely to scratch or damage the mouth or oesophagus.

Saliva's second job is to start breaking down fatty and starchy foods. Even though saliva is mostly water, it also contains some **enzymes**. These enzymes start breaking down certain types of food before they have even reached the stomach! This makes it easier for the rest of the digestive system to absorb the nutrients out of the food.

OVER **99%** of **SALIVA** is just **WATER.**

Epiglottis

This flap of **tissue**, called the epiglottis, stops food from going into the lungs.

Route
OESOPHAGUS:
HIGHWAY to the STOMACH

The oesophagus plays a very important role in the digestive system - it takes chewed up food from the mouth and transports it to the stomach. The oesophagus is also sometimes called the food pipe.

MUSCLE YOUR WAY IN

Unlike real pipes, the oesophagus is made out of muscles. Muscles are bundles of tissue that can squeeze together or relax. All animals have muscles in their bodies and people use muscles to do everything from walking to talking.

Some muscles, like the ones in the arms and legs, can be moved whenever we want. Other muscles, like the ones in the oesophagus, move without us even knowing. The muscles in the oesophagus help to push food towards the stomach.

It takes about **SEVEN SECONDS** for food to reach your **STOMACH** after it has been **SWALLOWED.**

SPHINCTER PASS

The oesophagus doesn't just open up straight into the stomach. Instead, before the food reaches the stomach it goes through a sphincter. Sphincters are circular muscles that squeeze together to close off one part of the body from another.

All sphincters stay squeezed together and closed off until they need to open. The sphincter at the bottom of the oesophagus only opens when food is about to go into the stomach.

Stomach

Oesophagus

Sphincter

If the sphincter stays open for too long, **acid** from the stomach can get into the oesophagus. This can be painful as the acid in the stomach is very strong. This is what is happening when people say that they have heartburn.

Heartburn can be very painful but medicine is often able to help.

There are over **60 DIFFERENT TYPES** of **SPHINCTER** in the **HUMAN BODY.**

15

Super STOMACH

The next stop on our journey through the digestive system is the stomach! The stomach stores food before it moves on to the rest of the digestive system. The stomach is made out of stretchy muscles, meaning that the stomach shrinks when it is empty and stretches when it gets full.

Everyone knows that stomachs can rumble and grumble. These noises are caused by air moving around in your digestive system. However, they have nothing to do with being hungry.

There is always air moving around in your digestive system, but the noise it makes can only be heard when there is no food in your stomach. When your stomach is full, the food blocks the noise so that you can't hear any rumbling.

When your **STOMACH is EMPTY**, it is about the size of your **FIST**.

CAN YOU STOMACH IT?

The stomach also churns and mixes up food. The muscles in your stomach **contract** every twenty seconds. This mixes up everything that's in the stomach. By the time the food leaves the stomach, it will have changed into a liquid.

On average, it takes the stomach around three hours to break down food into liquid.

FRESHLY SQUEEZED GASTRIC JUICE

However, the stomach couldn't turn food into liquid without the help of some gastric juice. Gastric juice is a mixture of different acids and enzymes. It is made in glands in the stomach. The juice is very powerful and it can kill almost any **germ** that enters the stomach. It also breaks down food so that the nutrients can be absorbed later.

GASTRIC JUICE is strong enough to EAT THROUGH WOOD!

17

DIGESTION
Perfection

The next stop on the journey is the small intestine. However, before we check out the small intestine, let's have a look at the organs that help it to do its job.

LILLY-LIVERED

The liver is the biggest gland in the entire body and it is part of a lot of different systems in the body. This makes it one of the body's **vital organs**. The main thing that the liver does for the digestive system is produce bile. Bile helps the body to absorb fat, which is very important for keeping the body healthy.

PANCREAS STATION

The pancreas makes pancreatic juice. This helps the body to break down proteins and carbohydrates and absorb their nutrients.

GALLBLADDER: THE LIVER'S BEST FRIEND

The liver is always making bile, but sometimes the small intestine doesn't need it. When this happens, the bile is stored in the gallbladder. While the bile is being stored, the gallbladder makes it more concentrated. This means that it takes water out of the bile so that it becomes stronger and can break down fat more easily.

Sometimes **GALLBLADDERS** have to be **REMOVED**. This is okay as humans can carry on living **WITHOUT** their gallbladders.

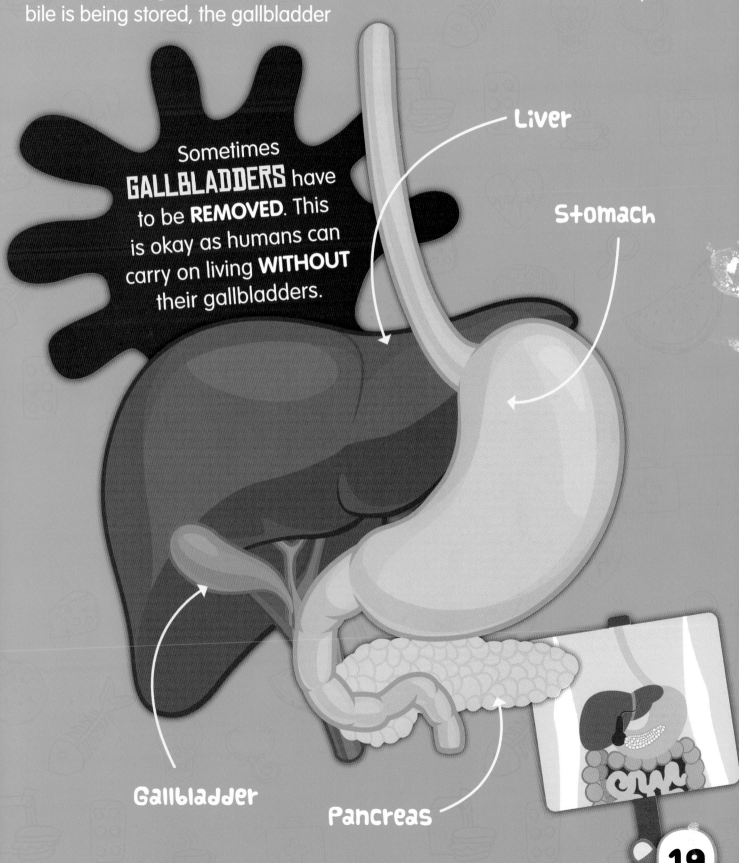

Liver

Stomach

Gallbladder

Pancreas

Great Things
COME IN SMALL
INTESTINE

After food has been turned into a liquid in the stomach, it enters the small intestine. The small intestine is where most of the food gets digested and nearly all the nutrients get absorbed. This makes it possibly the most important organ in the entire digestive system.

The small intestine is a long, thin tube that is around three centimetres wide and seven metres long. The small intestine is only able to fit inside the body because it is folded up and squished together.

Your **abdomen** is mostly taken up by the the **SMALL INTESTINE.**

I'M TOTALLY ABSORBED

When food leaves the small intestine, around 90% of its nutrients will have been absorbed by the body. Nearly all of these nutrients will have been absorbed by the small intestine.

When food enters the small intestine, it mixes with bile from the liver and pancreatic juice from the pancreas. On top of this, the small intestine makes more digestive juices of its own.

Once the food has been mixed with all of these juices and it has been broken down as much as possible, the small intestine is able to start absorbing the food's nutrients.

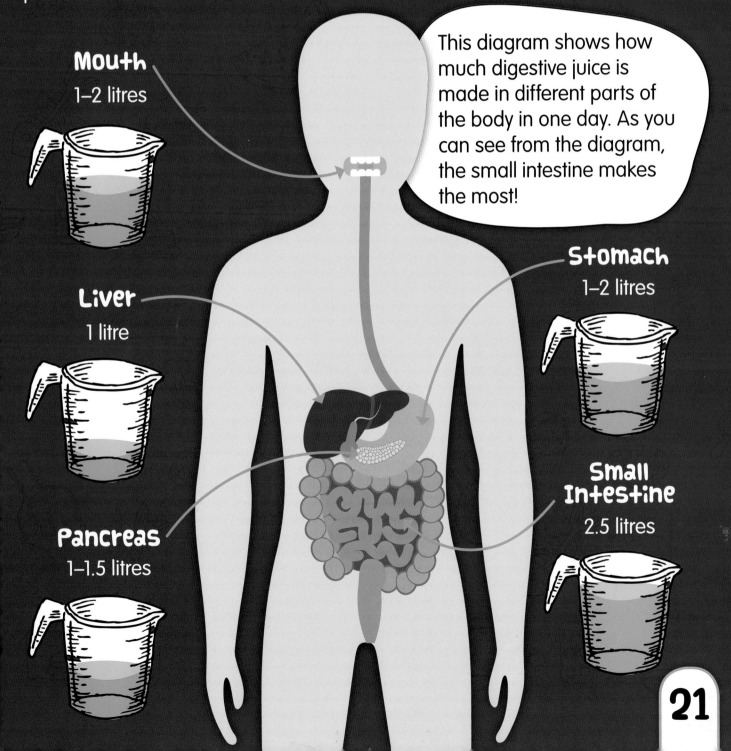

Mouth
1–2 litres

This diagram shows how much digestive juice is made in different parts of the body in one day. As you can see from the diagram, the small intestine makes the most!

Liver
1 litre

Stomach
1–2 litres

Pancreas
1–1.5 litres

Small Intestine
2.5 litres

COLON Farewell

Sadly, we are nearly at the end of our journey. But it's not time to say goodbye yet! We still have to go through the colon.

The colon goes all the way around the outside of the small intestine. The colon is also called the large intestine. It is only one and a half metres long, which means that it is actually shorter than the small intestine. The reason that the colon is called the large intestine is because it is between seven and eight centimetres wide – that's nearly three times wider than the small intestine!

Mouth and throat
10 cm

Oesophagus
25 cm

Stomach
25 cm

Small intestine
700 cm

Large intestine
150 cm

This diagram shows you the length of each part of the digestive tract.

Rectum
15 cm

UNCHARTED WATERS

When food reaches the colon, it has almost no nutrients left in it. However, it is still very watery. The main job of the large intestine is to absorb this water so that it can be used by the body.

THINGS THAT GO TRUMP IN THE NIGHT

The colon contains more **bacteria** than you could possibly imagine. There are more bacteria in the colon than there are stars in the night sky. Way, way more. But this is a good thing!

The bacteria in the colon can break down food even further so that the last few nutrients can be absorbed. However, the bacteria also make **gas**. This gas has to leave the body somehow – the more polite people out there might know this as passing wind.

WHAT GOES IN, Must COME OUT

Food that leaves the colon has been through a lot. It has travelled nine metres through the body. It has been mixed up and broken down. It has also had all of the nutrients and water sucked out of it. It has been squeezed, squished and smooshed to the point that it doesn't look anything like food any more. That's why the stuff that leaves the colon isn't called food. It's called poo or faeces.

ENGAGED

The final stop on our tour is the rectum. In humans, the rectum is usually only between ten and fifteen centimetres long. This makes it one of the shortest parts of the digestive system.

The faeces stays in the rectum until the rectum is nearly full. At this point, the body will let you know that you need to go to the toilet. The rest of the digestion process happens all on its own. But once the faeces reaches the rectum and needs to be gotten rid of, it's up to you.

Colon

Rectum

PEW POO!

We all know that faeces smells bad. This is because the bacteria in the colon give off nasty smells. However, if your faeces smells worse than normal, it might mean that you've eaten something that has upset your digestive system.

It takes **FOOD** about **72 HOURS** to go through the **DIGESTIVE SYSTEM** and leave the body as **FAECES**.

You CHEWS-You Lose

Sometimes, people feel pain in their stomach, small intestine or colon. This pain can be caused by a lot of different things. If you have pain in your abdomen and stomach area, it is always best to see a doctor.

A doctor can help when you have pains in your stomach.

Between **65%** and **75%** of people will find it **DIFFICULT** to **DIGEST DAIRY.**

Trust me, we're very clever!

SCARY DAIRY

One of the most common reasons why people have pains in their stomach is because they are lactose intolerant. Being lactose intolerant means that you have trouble digesting dairy. Dairy is its own food group and it contains foods that are made from milk. Butter, cheese and cream are all a part of the dairy food group. Babies are supposed to drink milk, but as people get older their bodies find it harder to digest dairy.

All of these things contain dairy and might make your stomach hurt if you are lactose intolerant.

GREASY AND UNEASY

Eating food that is very greasy can also make your stomach hurt. Fatty and greasy foods are the hardest to digest. This means that your digestive system has to work very hard when you eat a lot of greasy food. This can cause your stomach and small intestine to become **inflamed** and sore.

These foods all contain a lot of fat and grease. Eating lots of these foods is bad for you and can make you feel unwell.

The body needs some fat to stay healthy. However, too much fat is very bad for the body. Eating lots of fatty foods can make a person gain weight.

STOMACH Statistics

1. The average adult eats about 680 kilograms of food every year. That's the same weight as a cow.

9 metres

2.

An adult's stomach can hold up to 1.5 litres of food and liquid inside of it.

5 metres

3. If you stretched out an adult's digestive tract, it would be over 9 metres tall. This is about twice the height of a giraffe.

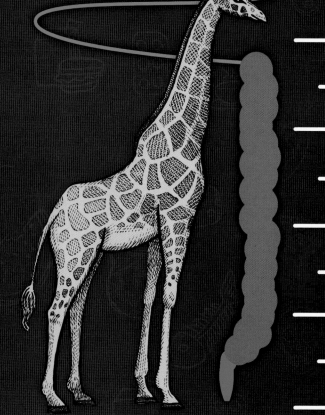

4.

It takes around 72 hours for food to go all the way through the human digestive system. This is about how long it took Neil Armstrong to get to the Moon in 1969.

5.

Muscles in the oesophagus push food towards your stomach. This means that you can still swallow food even when you are upside down.

6.

Some animals have many different parts to their stomach. This makes it easier for them to break down food. A cow's stomach has four parts to it.

DIGESTING Testing

Use what you've just learnt to try to answer these questions. The answers are upside down at the bottom of the page.

1. Which three organs help the small intestine to do its job?

2. How long does it take for the stomach to turn food into liquid?

3. What are the three types of teeth?

4. What is it in saliva that breaks down food in the mouth?

5. How many different types of sphincter are there in the human body?

6. What is the longest organ in the digestive tract?

7. What do we call people who have trouble digesting dairy?

8. Which food group is the body's main source of energy?

9. How big is a person's stomach when it is empty?

10. What do we call it when acid from the stomach gets into the oesophagus?

Answers: 1. Liver, gallbladder and pancreas 2. Three hours 3. Incisors, canines and molars 4. Enzymes 5. Over 60 6. Small intestine 7. Lactose intolerant 8. Starchy foods 9. The same size as their fist 10. Heartburn

GLOSSARY

abdomen — also called the tummy, it is the part of the body where most of the digestive organs can be found

absorbs — takes in or soaks up

acid — a type of chemical that can burn through materials if it is very strong

bacteria — extremely tiny living things that can either be very helpful or very harmful to the body

carbohydrates — foods that give us energy and contain sugar and starch

contract — squeeze together and become tighter

enzymes — substances made by living things that help the body in lots of ways, such as by breaking down food

gas — an air-like substance that can float around a room and often can't be seen

germ — an extremely tiny living organism that can make people ill

inflamed — swollen and sore

nutrients — natural substances that people need to grow and stay healthy

organs — parts of the body that have their own specific jobs or functions

saliva — a watery liquid made by glands in the mouth

systems — sets of things that work together to do specific jobs

tissue — any type of material that a living thing is made out of, including humans

vital organs — organs inside the body that are essential to our survival

INDEX